Welcome, Junior Explorer!

Your mission: open your eyes, explore every page, and collect the knowledge that will make you a true World Explorer.

Are you ready? Adventure awaits!

Welcome, Junior Explorer!

Hello, brave explorer! You are about to embark on a thrilling journey across the continents, discovering countries, capitals, mountains, rivers, and the world's incredible wonders."

Along the way, you'll uncover amazing facts, solve fun puzzles, and even earn your very own Junior Explorer Badge!

Your mission: open your eyes, explore every page, and collect the knowledge that will make you a true World Explorer.

Are you ready? Adventure awaits!

Your Explorer Map 🗺️

Here's your map of the world your playground of adventures! Every continent has secrets to uncover, from the icy mountains of Antarctica to the deserts of Africa, the rainforests of South America, and the colorful cities of Asia.

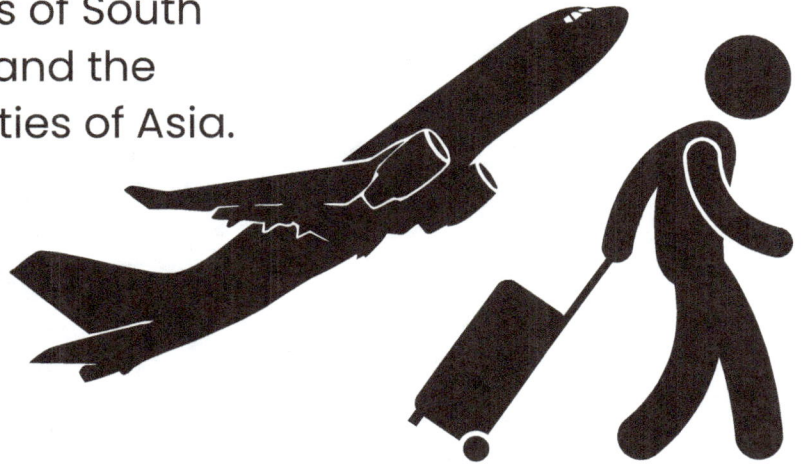

Your Junior Explorer Badge

How to Use This Book & Your Badge

- Complete each chapter to earn new "Explorer Points."
- Color maps, match countries to capitals, and complete mini-games to unlock special fun facts.
- By the end, you'll have earned your Junior Explorer Badge, proving you are a master of the world!

TITLE	LINE FOR CHILD TO WRITE
Explorer Name:	_____ _____
Mission Date:	_____ _____
I Will Go To: (My Dream Destination)	_____ _____

TITLE	LINE FOR CHILD TO WRITE
Explorer Name:	_____ _____
Mission Date:	_____ _____
I Will Go To: (My Dream Destination)	_____ _____

TITLE	LINE FOR CHILD TO WRITE
Explorer Name:	_____ _____
Mission Date:	_____ _____
I Will Go To: (My Dream Destination)	_____ _____

OFFICIAL JUNIOR EXPLORER LOG

1. Mission Tracker: The Continent Checklist
This is the main progress bar. Each continent box is left blank for the explorer to place a sticker, draw an X, or create your own official stamp once you've finished the chapter.

Continent	Status (Check/Stamp Here)	Favorite Fact Learned
🌍 **Africa** (54 Countries)	(Large Square Box)	_____ ____
🌏 **Asia** (48 Countries)	(Large Square Box)	_____ ____
🌍 **Europe** (44 Countries)	(Large Square Box)	_____ ____
🌎 **North America** (23 Countries)	(Large Square Box)	_____ ____
🌎 **South America** (12 Countries)	(Large Square Box)	_____ ____
🌏 **Oceania** (14 Countries)	(Large Square Box)	_____ ____
🌍 **Antarctica** (1 Country/Region)	(Large Square Box)	_____ ____

.JUNIOR EXPLORER BADGE TRACKER

Collect 100 Explorer Points to achieve your final Certificate!
Color in a badge below every time you earn 20 Explorer
Points!

[SHIELD/CIRCLE 1]	[SHIELD/CIRCLE 2]	[SHIELD/CIRCLE 3]	[SHIELD/CIRCLE 4]	[SHIELD/CIRCLE 5]
20 PTS	40 PTS	60 PTS	80 PTS	100 PTS

Chapter 1

Explore the Continents

The world is made up of 7 amazing continents, each filled with incredible animals, foods, mountains, rivers, and people! Get ready to travel from icy Antarctica to the deserts of Africa, the jungles of South America, and the bustling cities of Asia.

🌎 Africa (54 countries)

Algeria - Algiers
Angola - Luanda
Benin - Porto-Novo
Botswana - Gaborone
Burkina Faso -
Ouagadougou
Burundi - Gitega
Cabo Verde - Praia
Cameroon - Yaoundé
Central African Republic
-Bangui

Chad –-N'Djamena
Comoros - Moroni
Democratic Republic of
the Congo - Kinshasa
Republic of the Congo –
Brazzaville
Djibouti - Djibouti
Egypt - Cairo
Equatorial Guinea -
Malabo
Eritrea - Asmara

🌍 Africa (54 countries)

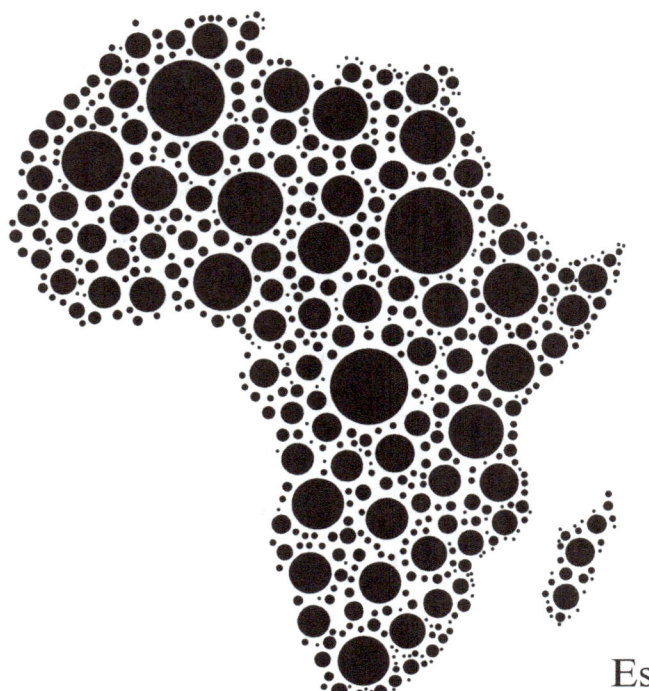

Kenya - Nairobi
Lesotho - Maseru
Liberia - Monrovia
Libya - Tripoli
Madagascar - Antananarivo
Malawi - Lilongwe
Mali –-Bamako
Mauritania - Nouakchott
Mauritius - Port Louis
Morocco - Rabat
Mozambique - Maputo

Eswatini - Mbabane
(administrative),
Lobamba (legislative)
Ethiopia - Addis
Ababa
Gabon - Libreville
Gambia - Banjul
Ghana - Accra
Guinea - Conakry
Guinea-Bissau - Bissau
Ivory Coast (Côte
d'Ivoire) –
Yamoussoukro
(official), Abidjan
(economic)

🌎 Africa (54 countries)

Namibia - Windhoek
Niger - Niamey
Nigeria - Abuja
Rwanda - Kigali
São Tomé and Príncipe -
São Tomé
Senegal - Dakar
Seychelles - Victoria
Sierra Leone - Freetown
Somalia - Mogadishu

South Africa - Pretoria
(administrative),
Bloemfontein (judicial),
Cape Town (legislative)
South Sudan - Juba
Sudan - Khartoum
Tanzania - Dodoma
Togo - Lomé
Tunisia - Tunis
Uganda - Kampala
Zambia - Lusaka
Zimbabwe - Harare

🌍 Asia (49 countries)

Afghanistan - Kabul

Armenia - Yerevan

Azerbaijan - Baku

Bahrain - Manama

Bangladesh - Dhaka

Bhutan - Thimphu

Brunei - Bandar Seri
Begawan

Cambodia - Phnom Penh

China - Beijing

Cyprus - Nicosia

Georgia - Tbilisi

India - New Delhi

Indonesia - Jakarta

Iran - Tehran

Iraq - Baghdad

🌍 Asia (49 countries)

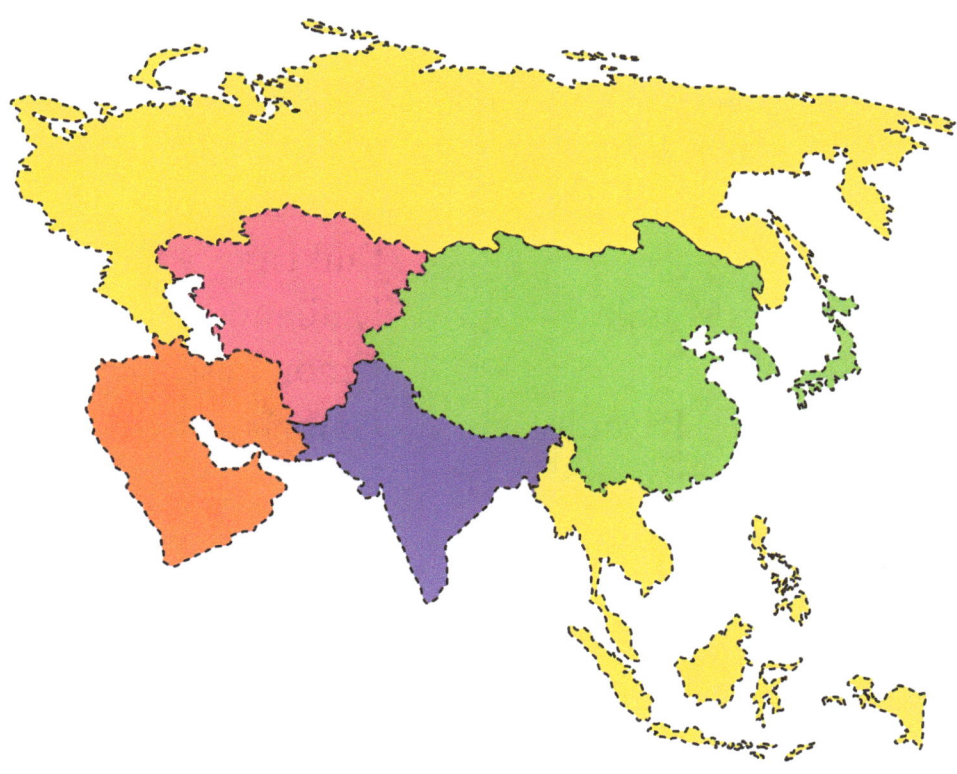

Israel - Jerusalem
Japan - Tokyo
Jordan - Amman
Kazakhstan - Astana
(Nur-Sultan, renamed
back to Astana in
2022)
Kuwait - Kuwait City
Kyrgyzstan – Bishkek
Laos - Vientiane
Lebanon - Beirut

Malaysia - Kuala
Lumpur
Maldives - Malé
Mongolia -
Ulaanbaatar
Myanmar (Burma) -
Naypyidaw
Nepal - Kathmandu
North Korea -
Pyongyang
Oman - Muscat

🌍 Asia (49 countries)

Oman – Muscat
Pakistan – Islamabad
Palestine – East Jerusalem (disputed, UN observer state)
Philippines – Manila
Qatar – Doha
Saudi Arabia – Riyadh
Singapore – Singapore
South Korea – Seoul
Sri Lanka – Sri Jayawardenepura Kotte (legislative), Colombo (commercial)
Syria – Damascus

Taiwan* – Taipei (*disputed, not UN-recognized as separate from China)
Tajikistan – Dushanbe
Thailand – Bangkok
Timor-Leste (East Timor) – Dili
Turkey – Ankara
Turkmenistan – Ashgabat
United Arab Emirates – Abu Dhabi
Uzbekistan – Tashkent
Vietnam – Hanoi
Yemen – Sana'a

🌍 Europe (44 countries)

Albania – Tirana
Andorra – Andorra la Vella
Austria – Vienna
Belarus – Minsk
Belgium – Brussels
Bosnia and Herzegovina – Sarajevo
Bulgaria – Sofia

Croatia – Zagreb
Czech Republic (Czechia) – Prague
Denmark – Copenhagen
Estonia – Tallinn
Finland – Helsinki
France – Paris
Germany – Berlin
Greece – Athens

🌍 Europe (44 countries)

Greece - Athens
Hungary - Budapest
Iceland - Reykjavik
Ireland - Dublin
Italy - Rome
Kosovo - Pristina
(*partially recognized,
UN disputed)
Latvia - Riga
Liechtenstein - Vaduz

Lithuania - Vilnius
Luxembourg -
Luxembourg
Malta - Valletta
Moldova - Chișinău
Monaco - Monaco
Montenegro - Podgorica
Netherlands -
Amsterdam

🌍 Europe (44 countries)

North Macedonia - Skopje
Norway - Oslo
Poland - Warsaw
Portugal - Lisbon
Romania - Bucharest
Russia - Moscow
San Marino - San Marino

Serbia - Belgrade
Slovakia - Bratislava
Slovenia - Ljubljana
Spain - Madrid
Sweden - Stockholm
Switzerland - Bern
Ukraine - Kyiv
United Kingdom - London

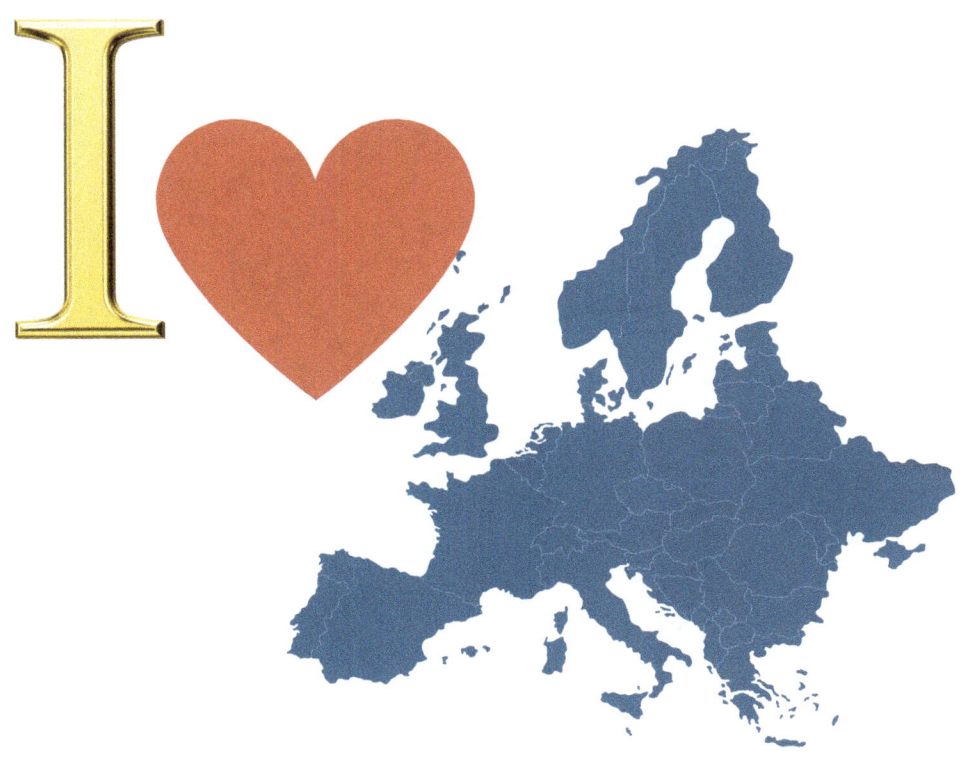

🌎 North America (23 countries)

Antigua and Barbuda - St. John's

Bahamas - Nassau

Barbados - Bridgetown

Belize - Belmopan

Canada - Ottawa

Costa Rica - San José

Cuba - Havana

Dominica - Roseau

Dominican Republic - Santo Domingo

El Salvador - San Salvador

Grenada - St. George's

Guatemala - Guatemala City

🌎 North America (23 countries)

Haiti - Port-au-Prince
Honduras - Tegucigalpa
Jamaica - Kingston
Mexico - Mexico City
Nicaragua - Managua
Panama - Panama City
Saint Kitts and Nevis -
Basseterre

Saint Lucia - Castries
Saint Vincent and the
Grenadines - Kingstown
Trinidad and Tobago -
Port of Spain
United States -
Washington, D.C.

🌎 South America (12 countries)

Argentina - Buenos Aires
Bolivia - Sucre (constitutional), La Paz (administrative/government)
Brazil - Brasília
Chile - Santiago
Colombia - Bogotá
Ecuador - Quito
Guyana - Georgetown
Paraguay - Asunción
Peru - Lima
Suriname - Paramaribo
Uruguay - Montevideo
Venezuela - Caracas

🌏 Oceania (14 countries)

Australia - Canberra
Fiji - Suva
Kiribati - South Tarawa
Marshall Islands - Majuro
Micronesia - Palikir
Nauru - Yaren District (de facto)
New Zealand - Wellington
Palau - Ngerulmud
Papua New Guinea - Port Moresby
Samoa - Apia
Solomon Islands - Honiara
Tonga - Nuku'alofa
Tuvalu - Funafuti
Vanuatu - Port Vila

🌍 Junior Explorer Badge Quiz – Chapter 1: Continents & Countries

1. How many continents are there in the world?

a) 5
b) 6
c) 7
d) 8

2. Which continent is the largest by land area?
a) Africa
b) Asia
c) Europe
d) South America

3. Which continent is also a country?

a) Antarctica
b) Asia
c) Australia
d) North America

4. True or False: Africa has the most countries of any continent.

5. Which continent is known as the "Frozen Land" because it's covered in ice?

a) North America
b) Antarctica
c) Europe
d) South America

6. The Amazon Rainforest is located on which continent?

a) Asia
b) South America
c) Africa
d) Australia

7. Which continent is home to the world's tallest mountain, Mount Everest?

a) Africa
b) Asia
c) Europe
d) North America

8. True or False: Europe is bigger than South America.

9. If you're standing in Cairo, Egypt, which continent are you on?
a) Asia
b) Africa
c) Europe
d) South America

10. Which continent is sometimes called the "Land Down Under"?
a) South America
b) Australia
c) Asia
d) Africa

⭐ **Fun Fact: People call it that because it's located in the Southern Hemisphere, "down under" most of the world's maps.**

✅ Junior Explorer Quiz – Answer Key + Fun Facts

1. How many continents are there in the world?

✔ Answer: 7

🌟 Fun Fact: Did you know that some people used to count only 6? Europe and Asia together were called Eurasia!

2. Which continent is the largest by land area?

✔ Answer: Asia

🌟 Fun Fact: Asia is so big it's larger than the Moon's surface!

3. Which continent is also a country?

✔ Answer: Australia

🌟 Fun Fact: Australia is the only place where kangaroos and koalas live in the wild.

4. True or False: Africa has the most countries of any continent.

✔ Answer: True

🌟 Fun Fact: Africa has 54 countries—that's more than any other continent.

5. Which continent is known as the "Frozen Land"?

✔️ **Answer: Antarctica**
🌟 **Fun Fact: No one lives in Antarctica permanently—only scientists and penguins hang out there! 🐧**

6. The Amazon Rainforest is located on which continent?

✔️ **Answer: South America**
🌟 **Fun Fact: The Amazon is called "the lungs of the Earth" because it produces 20% of the world's oxygen.**

7. Which continent is home to Mount Everest?

✔️ **Answer: Asia**
🌟 **Fun Fact: Mount Everest grows about 4 millimeters taller every year because of moving tectonic plates!**

8. True or False: Europe is bigger than South America.

✓ Answer: False
⭐ Fun Fact: South America is almost twice as big as Europe—but Europe has more people living there.

9. If you're standing in Cairo, Egypt, which continent are you on?

✓ Answer: Africa
⭐ Fun Fact: Egypt is special—it connects Africa and Asia through the Sinai Peninsula.

10. Which continent is called the "Land Down Under"?
✓ Answer: Australia

Chapter 2

Wonders of the World

✨ Welcome, Junior Explorer! ✨

The world is full of mysteries, magic, and breathtaking places built by humans and shaped by nature. These are called the Wonders of the World. Some are ancient treasures built thousands of years ago, while others are natural marvels so big and beautiful, they leave everyone in awe.

In this chapter, we'll travel together to see towering pyramids, temples carved into rock, gardens floating high above the ground, and even waterfalls that roar like thunder. 🌍 Each wonder has a story, a secret, and a special place on our Earth map.

Are you ready to unlock the secrets of the Wonders of the World and collect your Wonders Explorer Badge? 🏅 Pack your imagination—this journey begins now!

🌍 The Ancient Wonders of the World

A long, long time agobefore planes, cars, or even electricitypeople built amazing creations so incredible that travelers called them the "Seven Wonders of the World." These wonders were huge, mysterious, and so beautiful that they became legends.

Sadly, most of them disappeared over time because of earthquakes, wars, and weather. But their stories still live on, and one of them still stands tall today!
Let's go on a time-traveling adventure to meet these wonders!

🏜️ 1. The Great Pyramid of Giza (Egypt)

- The only ancient wonder still standing!
- Built over 4,500 years ago as a tomb for Pharaoh Khufu.

- **Fun Fact:** It was the tallest building in the world for more than 3,800 years!

🌱 2. The Hanging Gardens of Babylon (Iraq, maybe!)

- Said to be filled with trees, flowers, and waterfalls hanging high in the sky.
- Mystery: Historians aren't even sure they really existed!

- **Fun Fact:** Imagine a giant garden in the desert it would have been like magic!

⚡ 3. The Statue of Zeus (Olympia, Greece)

- A giant statue of the king of the Greek gods, Zeus, sitting on a golden throne.
- Built about 2,400 years ago.

- **Fun Fact**: It was as tall as a 4-story building!

🏛 4. The Temple of Artemis (Ephesus, Turkey)

- A massive temple built for Artemis, the Greek goddess of the hunt.
- Rebuilt many times after being destroyed.

- **Fun Fact:** It was said to be bigger than a football field!

🪦 5. The Mausoleum at Halicarnassus (Turkey)

- A giant tomb for King Mausolus and his queen.
- So famous that the word mausoleum (meaning fancy tomb) comes from it!

- **Fun Fact:** Decorated with 400 statues!

☀️ 6. The Colossus of Rhodes (Greece)

- change this pictures please honeymoon

- A bronze statue of the sun god Helios, standing as tall as the Statue of Liberty.
- Guarded the harbor of Rhodes.

- **Fun Fact:** Ships sailed between its legs (well, maybe that's the legend!).

💡 7. The Lighthouse of Alexandria (Egypt)

- One of the tallest buildings in the ancient world, guiding ships safely to shore.
- Built on Pharos Island.

- **Fun Fact:** It stood for 1,500 years before earthquakes knocked it down!

✨ End of Part 1:

Wasn't that amazing?

 Some of these wonders are lost forever, but their stories remind us of how creative and determined people were thousands of years ago.

Next up... the New Seven Wonders of the World and guess what? You can still visit them today!

✨ The New Seven Wonders of the World

Time to fast-forward to the present!

In 2007, people all around the world voted to choose the New Seven Wonders of the World. These are amazing places that still exist today you could visit them if you wanted! Each one has a story, a secret, and a "wow" factor that makes it unforgettable.

Let's pack our explorer backpacks and see them one by one!

🧱 1. The Great Wall of China (China)

- A wall so long it stretches over 13,000 miles!
- Built to protect ancient China from invasions.

- **Fun Fact:** It's not visible from space with the naked eye (sorry, that's a myth!), but it's still the longest wall in the world.

🏜️🌵 2. Petra (Jordan)

- An ancient city carved into pink and red rock cliffs.
- Known as the "Rose City" because of its color.

- **Fun Fact:** The famous building called "The Treasury" looks like a giant palace carved by hand.

✝️ 3. Christ the Redeemer (Brazil)

- A giant statue of Jesus standing high above Rio de Janeiro.
- Built in 1931 and standing 98 feet tall with arms wide open.

- **Fun Fact:** The statue's arms stretch 92 feet wide almost the length of a Boeing 737 airplane!

⛰️ 4. Machu Picchu (Peru)

- An ancient Inca city hidden in the Andes Mountains.
- Built over 500 years ago and abandoned for centuries.

- **Fun Fact:** It's sometimes called the "Lost City of the Incas" because no one knew about it until 1911!

☀️ 5. Chichen Itza (Mexico)

- A huge pyramid built by the Maya people around 1,500 years ago.
- Known as El Castillo ("The Castle").

- **Fun Fact:** During the spring and fall equinox, the shadow of a snake seems to slither down the steps spooky and amazing!

🏟️ 6. The Roman Colosseum (Italy)

- A massive arena in Rome where gladiators once battled.
- Could seat over 50,000 spectators!

- **Fun Fact:** It had trapdoors, elevators, and secret tunnels like an ancient sports stadium with special effects.

💎 7. The Taj Mahal (India)

- A beautiful white marble palace built by Emperor Shah Jahan for his wife Mumtaz.
- Called a "monument of love."

- **Fun Fact:** The color of the Taj Mahal changes depending on the time of day pink in the morning, white in the afternoon, and golden under the moonlight.

✨ End of Part 2

From the lost cities of Petra and Machu Pic chu to the shining beauty of the Taj Mahal, these wonders remind us that the world is full of magic, history, and love.

Who knows? Maybe one day you'll stand in front of one of them with your own eyes! 🌍

🌍 **Junior Explorer Badge Quiz – Chapter 2**

Explorer, it's time to test your knowledge! Answer these questions to see if you've earned your "Wonders Explorer Badge."

1. 🌍 Which ancient wonder is the only one still standing today?

   1. a) Statue of Zeus
   2. b) Great Pyramid of Giza
   3. c) Lighthouse of Alexandria

2. 🌱 The Hanging Gardens of Babylon might not have really existed. True or False?

3. ⚡ The Statue of Zeus was as tall as a:
   1. a) 2-story house
   2. b) 4-story building
   3. c) 10-story skyscraper

4. 🏛 The word mausoleum (a fancy tomb) comes from which ancient wonder?

5. 💡 The Lighthouse of Alexandria helped:
  - a) Farmers grow crops
  - b) Ships find their way to shore
  - c) People see in the dark

6. 🧱 Which New Wonder is more than 13,000 miles long?

7. ⛰️ Which New Wonder is hidden high in the Andes Mountains of Peru?

8. ✝️ The Christ the Redeemer statue in Brazil has arms almost as wide as:

  a) A car
  - b) A school bus
c) An airplane

9. ☀️ At Chichen Itza, what animal seems to slither down the pyramid during the equinox?

10. 💎 The Taj Mahal was built as a symbol of:

a) War
b) Love
c) Wealth

Junior Explorer Badge Quiz

answers

🌍 **Which ancient wonder is the only one still standing today?**

a) Statue of Zeus
b) Great Pyramid of Giza ✅
c) Lighthouse of Alexandria

🌿 **The Hanging Gardens of Babylon might not have really existed. True or False?**
Answer: True ✅

⚡ **The Statue of Zeus was as tall as a:**
a) 2-story house
b) 4-story building ✅
c) 10-story skyscraper

🏛 **The word mausoleum (a fancy tomb) comes from which ancient wonder?**
Answer: Mausoleum at Halicarnassus ✅

💡 **The Lighthouse of Alexandria helped:**
a) Farmers grow crops
b) Ships find their way to shore ✅
c) People see in the dark

🧱 **Which New Wonder is more than 13,000 miles long?**
Answer: The Great Wall of China ✅

🏔 **Which New Wonder is hidden high in the Andes Mountains of Peru?**
Answer: Machu Picchu ✅

✝️ **The Christ the Redeemer statue in Brazil has arms almost as wide as:**
a) A car
b) A school bus
c) An airplane ✅

☀️ **At Chichen Itza, what animal seems to slither down the pyramid during the equinox?**
Answer: A serpent / snake ✅

💎 **The Taj Mahal was built as a symbol of:**
a) War
b) Love ✅
c) Wealth

🌿 5 of the World's Most Beautiful National Parks

National parks are nature's treasures – gifts from the Earth filled with amazing animals, colorful birds, towering trees, sparkling rivers, and breathtaking landscapes. 🌿🦁

These protected lands let us step into a world of wonder, where every corner is an adventure waiting to be discovered. From roaring waterfalls to endless plains, each park has its own story, secrets, and magic.

Get ready, Junior Explorer! 🧭 Here are 5 of the most beautiful national parks in the world, each one a place where nature shines its brightest and adventure never ends.

🦁 1. Serengeti National Park (Tanzania, Africa)

- Known as the "Endless Plains," the Serengeti is home to one of the most breathtaking events in nature: the Great Migration.

- Every year, millions of wildebeest, zebras, and gazelles travel across the plains in search of fresh grass.

- **Fun Fact:** The word Serengeti comes from the Maasai language and means "endless land."

🐻 2. Yellowstone National Park (United States, North America)

- The first national park in the world (created in 1872)!
- Famous for its bubbling hot springs, exploding geysers (like Old Faithful), and rainbow-colored pools.
- Home to grizzly bears, bison, wolves, and elk.

- **Fun Fact:** Yellowstone sits on a super volcano–don't worry, it's sleeping!

🏔️ 3. Banff National Park (Canada, North America)

- Nestled in the Rocky Mountains, Banff is like a postcard come to life.
- With turquoise lakes, snowy peaks, and lush forests, it's one of the most photographed places in the world.

- **Fun Fact:** Lake Louise, inside Banff, is so blue it looks like someone spilled paint in it–but it's all natural!

🐘 4. Kruger National Park (South Africa, Africa)

- One of the best places to see Africa's Big Five: lions, leopards, elephants, rhinos, and buffalo.
- Stretching across nearly 7,500 square miles, it's bigger than the country of Israel!

- **Fun Fact:** Kruger has over 500 bird species—a paradise for bird lovers.

🌸 Fuji-Hakone-Izu National Park (Japan, Asia)

- Home to the iconic Mount Fuji, Japan's tallest and most sacred mountain.
- Known for its cherry blossoms, hot springs, and views so beautiful they look like paintings.

- **Fun Fact:** Mount Fuji is actually a volcano, but it's very peaceful now.

✨ Explorer's Tip:

National parks are treasures that protect nature, animals, and culture. Visiting them is like stepping into a real life adventure movie!

🌊 5 Longest Rivers in the World

🌊 5 Longest Rivers in the World

Rivers are the life veins of our planet winding through mountains, forests, deserts, and cities, carrying water, animals, and stories across continents. 🌿🐊

Some rivers are so long they seem to never end, and each one has its own secrets, adventures, and amazing wildlife waiting to be discovered. From the powerful rapids to peaceful stretches, rivers are nature's highways that connect the world!

Junior Explorer, grab your map and compass! 🧭 Here are 5 of the longest rivers in the world, each one a journey through history, nature, and the wonders of our planet.

Nile River (Africa) – 4,135 miles / 6,650 km

- The longest river in the world!
- Flows through 11 countries, including Egypt and Sudan, and ends in the Mediterranean Sea.
- Ancient Egyptians built their whole civilization around it farming, fishing, and traveling.

- 🌟 **Fun Fact:** Without the Nile, the pyramids and pharaohs' empire would never have existed!

Amazon River (South America) – 4,000 miles / 6,400 km

- The mightiest river by water volume it carries more water than any other river on Earth.
- Flows mainly through Brazil, winding through the Amazon Rainforest, the "lungs of the Earth."
- Home to pink river dolphins, piranhas, and the anaconda.

- 🌟 **Fun Fact:** Some places along the Amazon are so wide you can't see the other side!

Yangtze River (China, Asia) – 3,915 miles / 6,300 km

- The longest river in Asia.
- Flows entirely within China and is important for farming, transportation, and culture.
- Famous for the breathtaking Three Gorges and the mighty Three Gorges Dam

- ⭐ Fun Fact: The Yangtze is home to a unique animal called the Chinese giant salamander the world's largest amphibian!

Mississippi–Missouri River System (United States, North America) – 3,902 miles / 6,275 km

- Together, the Mississippi and Missouri Rivers form one of the world's longest river systems.
- The Mississippi is called the "Father of Waters" and has inspired songs, stories, and legends.
- Flows through the heart of America, from Minnesota to the Gulf of Mexico.

- 🌟 Fun Fact: Steamboats once ruled the Mississippi, carrying people and goods like floating hotels.

Yenisei River (Mongolia & Russia, Asia) – 3,445 miles / 5,539 km

- The largest river flowing into the Arctic Ocean.
- Starts in Mongolia, runs through Siberia, and empties into the icy Arctic waters.
- Its basin is wild and remote, home to Siberian tigers, reindeer, and snowy forests.

- 🌟 **Fun Fact:** Parts of the Yenisei stay frozen for almost half the year!

✨ Explorer's Thought:

Rivers are the Earth's lifelines. They carry water, stories, animals, and people connecting us all like nature's highways.

⛰️ The 5 Highest Mountains in the World

Mountains are Earth's giant guardians, reaching up to touch the sky and challenging every explorer who dares to climb them. ⛺✨

Some mountains are so tall, their summits seem to kiss the clouds, and each one has amazing stories, hidden secrets, and breathtaking views. From snowy peaks to icy ridges, mountains are nature's playgrounds and classrooms, teaching us about courage, patience, and the beauty of our planet.

Junior Explorer, get ready to strap on your boots and explore the world's highest mountains! Here are the 5 tallest peaks, each one waiting to amaze you with its height, history, and adventures.

Mount Everest (Nepal/China – Himalayas) – 29,032 ft / 8,849 m

- The highest mountain in the world!
- Lies in the Himalayas on the border between Nepal and Tibet (China).

- 🌟 **Fun Fact:** The summit is so high that climbers can see the curve of the Earth. Oxygen is very thin, making it one of the toughest climbs on Earth!

K2 (Pakistan/China – Karakoram Range) – 28,251 ft / 8,611 m

- Nicknamed the "Savage Mountain" because it's one of the hardest to climb.
- Located on the border between Pakistan and China.

- 🌟 **Fun Fact:** Fewer people have stood on K2's summit than on the moon! 🚀

Kangchenjunga (India/Nepal Himalayas) – 28,169 ft / 8,586 m

- The third-highest mountain in the world.
- Known as the "Five Treasures of the Snow" because of its five majestic peaks.

- ⭐ **Fun Fact:** For many years, explorers thought it was the tallest mountain until Everest was measured more accurately.

Lhotse (Nepal/China Himalayas)
27,940 ft / 8,516 m

- Right next to Mount Everest, often called its "neighbor."
- The climb is extremely challenging, with steep icy walls.

- 🌟 **Fun Fact:** In Tibetan, Lhotse means "South Peak."

Makalu (Nepal/China – Himalayas) – 27,838 ft / 8,485 m

- The fifth-highest mountain in the world.
- Famous for its pyramid-shaped peak that looks breathtaking from the sky.

- 🌟 **Fun Fact:** Because of its sharp ridges, climbers call it one of the most technically difficult peaks in the Himalayas.

✨ Explorer's Thought: Mountains are the Earth's giant guardians, reaching up to touch the sky. They challenge humans but also remind us how small we are in the vast world. 🌍💙

🏔 Highest Mountains by Continent

Junior Explorer, after learning about the world's top 5 mountains, it's time to meet the tallest mountains on each continent! These peaks are like nature's crowns, each with its own story and adventure.

🌍 Africa – Mount Kilimanjaro (Tanzania)
Height: 19,341 ft / 5,895 m

- Famous for being a free-standing mountain, not part of a range.
- **Fun Fact:** Climbers pass through five climate zones – from rainforest to glaciers all in one hike!
- **Badge:** 🌋 "Crown of Africa"

🌎 North America – Denali (Alaska, USA)

- Height: 20,310 ft / 6,190 m
- Tallest mountain in North America, covered in snow and ice almost year-round.

- **Fun Fact:** Its name "Denali" means "The High One" in the native Koyukon language.

- **Badge:** ❄️ "North Star Peak"

🌍 Europe Mount Elbrus (Russia)

- Height: 18,510 ft / 5,642 m
- Located in the Caucasus Mountains, often called Europe's highest peak.

- **Fun Fact:** It's actually a dormant volcano!
- **Badge:** 🌋 "European Volcano"

🌍 Antarctica – Mount Vinson (Antarctica)

- Height: 16,050 ft / 4,892 m
- The tallest mountain in the icy continent of Antarctica.

- **Fun Fact:** Only a few hundred climbers have ever reached the summit because it's so remote and cold!
- **Badge:** ❄️ "Frozen Giant"

🌏 Oceania – Puncak Jaya (Indonesia / New Guinea)

- Height: 16,024 ft / 4,884 m
- Tallest mountain in Oceania, part of the Sudirman Range.

- **Fun Fact:** It has tropical glaciers, which is rare for such a warm part of the world!
- **Badge:** 🌴 "Island Peak"

🌏 Bonus: Australia Mount Kosciuszko (Australia)

- Height: 7,310 ft / 2,228 m
- Tallest mountain in mainland Australia.

- **Fun Fact:** Much smaller than other continents' giants, but perfect for beginner climbers!
- **Badge:** 🐨 "Down Under Peak"

Remember

🌏 Mount Everest (Nepal/China)
Height: 29,032 ft / 8,849 m
The highest mountain in the world!
Badge: ⛰️ "Roof of the World"

Mount Kilimanjaro is considered the tallest free-standing mountain in the world and often called the tallest walkable (non-technical) mountain you can climb. 🌍🏔️

🌍 Africa – Kilimanjaro

🌎 North America – Denali

🌎 South America – Aconcagua

🌍 Europe – Elbrus

🌍 Antarctica – Vinson

🌏 Oceania – Puncak Jaya

🌏 Asia – Mount Everest

🌊 The 5 Deepest Lakes in the World

Lakes are hidden worlds of wonder, filled with sparkling waters, mysterious creatures, and secrets waiting to be discovered. 🌊✨

Some lakes are so deep they seem to touch the heart of the Earth, holding millions of years of history beneath their surfaces. From icy Antarctic lakes to warm African waters, each one is a home for amazing animals and plants, and a place where explorers can imagine incredible adventures.

Junior Explorer, grab your imaginary scuba gear! 🤿 Here are the 5 deepest lakes in the world, each one a watery kingdom full of magic, mystery, and adventure.

Lake Baikal (Russia – Siberia) 5,387 ft / 1,642 m

- The deepest lake in the world and the oldest, over 25 million years old!
- Holds 20% of the world's fresh water.

- **Fun Fact:** It's home to Baikal seals, the only freshwater seals in the world!
- **Badge:** ❄️ "Siberian Giant"

Lake Tanganyika (Africa – Tanzania/DR Congo/Burundi/Zambia) – 4,823 ft / 1,470 m

- The longest freshwater lake in the world (about 420 miles / 676 km).
- Home to over 350 species of fish found nowhere else!

- **Fun Fact:** Locals call it the "inland sea" because of its size and waves.
- **Badge:** 🌊 "African Giant"

Caspian Sea (Between Europe & Asia) – 3,363 ft / 1,025 m

- The largest enclosed body of water on Earth, often called a "sea" but really a giant lake.
- Surrounded by 5 countries: Russia, Kazakhstan, Turkmenistan, Iran, Azerbaijan.

- **Fun Fact:** Rich in history ancient traders on the Silk Road passed by it.
- **Badge:** 🌅 "Saltwater Giant"

Lake Vostok (Antarctica) – 3,300 ft / 1,000 m

- A hidden subglacial lake, buried under 2 miles (4 km) of ice.
- Mysterious and ancient isolated for millions of years.

- **Fun Fact:** Scientists believe it could host unknown life forms! 🧬
- **Badge:** ❄️ "Frozen Secret"

O'Higgins–San Martín Lake (Chile & Argentina) – 2,742 ft / 836 m

- Nestled in Patagonia, surrounded by glaciers and mountains.
- Known for its turquoise waters that change shades with the light.

- **Fun Fact:** Shared between two countries, it has two names depending on which side you visit!
- **Badge:** 🌈 "Patagonian Jewel"

🌟 Junior Explorer Challenge –

- Instructions: Write your answers in complete sentences. Think like a true explorer! ✨

- ## Highest Mountains

- a) Name the highest mountain in the world. Where is it located?
- b) Which mountain is the tallest free-standing (walkable) mountain in the world? Why is it special?
- c) Pick one of the world's top 5 mountains and describe one fun fact about it.

- ## Deepest Lakes

- a) What is the deepest lake in the world and which country is it in?
- b) Name two other very deep lakes and one interesting fact about each.

c) Why are some lakes like Lake Vostok so mysterious?

🌟 Junior Explorer Challenge

- **Longest Rivers**

- a) Which river is considered the longest in the world? Which continent is it on?
- b) Name one river that carries the most water in the world. What makes it special?
- c) Pick any river from the list of the 5 longest rivers and write a short sentence about one animal or plant that lives there.

- **National Parks**

- a) Name two national parks that you would love to visit. Why?
- b) What makes a national park different from other lands?
- c) Write a short paragraph explaining why we should protect national parks and the

- **animals that live there.**

- ✨ Explorer Tip: Draw a small picture of one mountain, lake, river, or national park you like the most on the back of your page! 🏞️🖌️

🌟 Mini Fact Sheets & Fun Boxes

Did You Know? Mountains

- Mount Everest grows about 4 mm taller every year because of shifting tectonic plates! 🌍
- Mount Kilimanjaro has 5 climate zones – from rainforest to icy summit – all in one hike. 🌿❄️

Did You Know? – Lakes

- Lake Baikal is over 25 million years old – the oldest freshwater lake in the world! ⏳
- Lake Tanganyika is so long (420 miles / 676 km) that it's sometimes called Africa's inland sea. 🌊
-

Did You Know? – Rivers

- The Amazon River produces about 20% of the world's fresh water that flows into oceans! 💧
- The Nile River is called the "Father of African Rivers" because ancient civilizations depended on it. 🏺

🌟 Mini Fact Sheets & Fun Boxes

Did You Know? – National Parks

- Serengeti National Park hosts the largest migration of land animals on Earth – millions of wildebeest, zebras, and gazelles! 🦓
- Yellowstone National Park has over 10,000 geothermal features, including geysers and hot springs! 🌋

Explorer Spotlight – Famous Explorers

1. Sir Edmund Hillary & Tenzing Norgay
   - First humans to reach the summit of Mount Everest in 1953.

   - **Fun Fact:** Tenzing was a Sherpa from Nepal, and Hillary was from New Zealand – teamwork made them unstoppable! 🏔️

2. Henry Morton Stanley
   - Explored Lake Tanganyika and the Congo River in Africa.

   - Fun Fact: He once greeted Dr. Livingstone with the famous words, **"Dr. Livingstone, I presume?"** 🌍

🌟 Mini Fact Sheets & Fun Boxes

3. Jacques Cousteau

- Famous for exploring oceans, lakes, and rivers around the world.
- Fun Fact: Invented the Aqua-Lung, making scuba diving possible for modern explorers! 🤿

4. John Muir
- Known as the Father of National Parks in the United States.
- Fun Fact: His love for Yosemite and the Sierra Nevada helped save them for future generations. 🌲

5. Alexandra Cousteau (modern explorer)
- Works to protect rivers and freshwater ecosystems worldwide.
- Fun Fact: She continues her family legacy of inspiring young explorers to care for water and wildlife. 💧

🌟 Mini Fact Sheets & Fun Boxes

Did You Know? Animals Around the World
- African Elephants can communicate through vibrations in the ground that humans can't feel! 🐘

- Peacocks spread their tail feathers to attract mates, but did you know they can also predict rain in some cultures? 🌈

Did You Know? Climates & Biomes
- The Sahara Desert can reach temperatures over 122°F / 50°C during the day! ☀️
- Antarctica is the coldest continent some places haven't seen rain or snow for millions of years! ❄️

Did You Know? Cultures & Places
- Machu Picchu in Peru was built in the 15th century and hidden from the outside world for hundreds of years. 🏔️

- The Great Wall of China is so long that it stretches across more than 13,000 miles that's like going around the Earth halfway!

🌟 Mini Fact Sheets & Fun Boxes

Explorer Spotlight – Female Explorers

- Dian Fossey studied gorillas in Rwanda and helped protect them from poachers. 🦍
- Freya Stark explored deserts and mountains in the Middle East and wrote amazing stories about her adventures. 🏜️

🔟 Explorer Challenge Box

- Can you draw your favorite mountain, river, lake, or national park and write one "Did You Know?" fact about it?
- Hint: Use the facts you learned from the book or make up a creative story as a Junior Explorer! 🖍️🗺️

Junior Explorer Puzzles & Activities

Maze:Help the Explorer Reach the Mountain Summit

- A winding mountain path maze with rocks, trees, and clouds.
- Goal: Trace the path from the base camp to the summit without hitting obstacles.
- Fun twist: Add mini "Did You Know?" facts along the path kids can read as they go.

Connect the Dots: Create the National Park Scene

- Kids connect numbered dots to reveal a lion, elephant, or waterfall in a park scene.
- After completing, they can color it in.
- Fun twist: Each dot could include a tiny fact – e.g., "Lions live in Serengeti!"

Junior Explorer Puzzles & Activities

Word Search: Geography Terms

- Words to find: River, Lake, Mountain, National Park, Summit, Glacier, Explorer, Jungle, Ocean, Desert
- Bonus: Include hidden words for specific names like Kilimanjaro, Baikal, Nile, Amazon, Everest.

Matching Game: Rivers, Lakes, Mountains, Parks

- Left column: Names (e.g., Nile, Kilimanjaro, Yellowstone, Baikal)
- Right column: Fun facts or country/continent
- Kids draw lines connecting the name to its description.

Spot the Difference: Two National Park Scenes

- Two nearly identical park illustrations.
- Kids must find 10 differences (e.g., missing tree, extra animal, different rock shape).
- Encourages observation skills and attention to detail.

Junior Explorer Puzzles & Activities

Word Search: Geography Terms

- Words to find: River, Lake, Mountain, National Park, Summit, Glacier, Explorer, Jungle, Ocean, Desert
- Bonus: Include hidden words for specific names like Kilimanjaro, Baikal, Nile, Amazon, Everest.

Matching Game: Rivers, Lakes, Mountains, Parks

- Left column: Names (e.g., Nile, Kilimanjaro, Yellowstone, Baikal)
- Right column: Fun facts or country/continent
- Kids draw lines connecting the name to its description.

Spot the Difference: Two National Park Scenes

- Two nearly identical park illustrations.
- Kids must find 10 differences (e.g., missing tree, extra animal, different rock shape).
- Encourages observation skills and attention to detail.

Junior Explorer Puzzles & Activities

Explorer Challenge Crossword

- Clues could be simple and geography-themed:

  "Tallest mountain in the world" → Everest
  "Deepest lake" → Baikal
  "Longest river" → Nile or Amazon
  "Park famous for geysers" → Yellowstone

- Can include small illustrations in some squares for fun hints.

A "Draw Your Favorite Adventure"

Congratulations, Junior Explorer! 🏅 You've traveled across mountains, rivers, lakes, and national parks, discovering amazing facts and hidden wonders of our world.
Now it's your turn to create your very own adventure! 🌍✨

- Imagine the place you would love to explore.

- Draw the mountains you would climb, the rivers you would sail, or the animals you would meet.

- Add trees, flowers, animals, or even a hidden treasure anything your explorer heart dreams of!

There are no limits your adventure is as big and magical as your imagination. 🌈
Grab your colors, pencils, or markers, and bring your journey to life!

Your Adventure Awaits... Draw It Here:

EXPLORER'S FIELD NOTES & QUICK SKETCH

Deserts:

Five Deserts: The Sand, The Ice, and The Stars
Here are some facts about five of the world's
most amazing deserts places that are defined
not just by sand, but by extreme heat, cold,
and incredible hidden life.

1. The Sahara Desert

Where it is: North Africa. It covers an absolutely huge area, stretching across 11 different countries, from the Red Sea coast to the Atlantic Ocean.

Special Thing: The Sahara isn't just a sand pit! It's the largest hot desert in the world, but it experiences huge, sudden temperature changes. At night, the temperature can drop from scorching hot down to freezing cold in just a few hours. Scientists also believe the Sahara shifts its boundaries and actually "breathes," growing larger during the dry season and shrinking slightly when the rains arrive.

2. The Kalahari Desert

Where it is: Southern Africa. It mainly covers
Botswana, Namibia, and South Africa.
Special Thing: People call the Kalahari a
"thirstland" rather than a true desert because it
actually gets more rainfall than places like the
Sahara. Its ground is covered in rusty red sand
that stays fixed thanks to sparse but deep-rooted
grasses. This allows for vast herds of wildlife, like
giraffes and meerkats, to live there, making it an
incredibly unique wildlife habitat.

3. The Gobi Desert

Where it is: Asia. It stretches across vast areas of northern China and southern Mongolia.
Special Thing: This is the most famous cold winter desert on Earth! Unlike hot deserts, the Gobi regularly freezes, with temperatures plunging far below zero. It's also one of the most important places for dinosaur fossils. Paleontologists have found perfectly preserved dinosaur eggs and skeletons here that have given us huge clues about ancient life.

4. The Arabian Desert

Where it is: Southwest Asia. It covers almost the entire Arabian Peninsula, including Saudi Arabia, Yemen, Oman, and several other countries.
Special Thing: The Arabian Desert contains the Rub' al Khali (or "Empty Quarter"), which is the largest continuous body of sand in the world. It's a spectacular place known for its massive, high, red-orange sand dunes that can reach heights of over 800 feet, making it look like a giant, wind-sculpted maze.

5. The Atacama Desert

- Where it is: South America, primarily running along the coast of Chile.
- Special Thing: The Atacama is famous for being the driest non-polar desert in the world. Some parts are so barren and dry that they haven't recorded any significant rainfall for hundreds of years! Because the air is so clean and dry, it's the perfect spot for astronomers. Some of the world's most powerful telescopes are built here, allowing us to see the stars clearer than almost anywhere else.

🖍️ Junior Explorer Drawing Guide

Use this checklist to make your adventure magical, fun, and full of wonder! You can include:

🏞️ Landscape & Nature

- Tall mountains 🏔️

- Sparkling rivers 🌊

- Deep lakes 🌊

- Forests and trees 🌳🌲

- Beaches or deserts 🌵

🐾 Animals & Wildlife

- Lions, elephants, zebras 🦁🐘🦓

- Birds and butterflies 🦋🦜

- Whales, fish, or sea creatures 🐟🐠

- Any imaginary animals you dream up! ✨

🖍️ Junior Explorer Drawing Guide

Use this checklist to make your adventure magical, fun, and full of wonder! You can include:

🏞️ Landscape & Nature
- Tall mountains 🏔️
- Sparkling rivers 🌊
- Deep lakes 🌊
- Forests and trees 🌳🌲
- Beaches or deserts 🏜️

🐾 Animals & Wildlife
- Lions, elephants, zebras 🦁🐘🦓
- Birds and butterflies 🦋🦜
- Whales, fish, or sea creatures 🐟🐠
- Any imaginary animals you dream up! ✨

🧭 Explorers & Adventure
- Yourself as a Junior Explorer 🧒🧑
- Compass, backpack, or binoculars 🧭🎒🔭
- Hidden treasures or secret caves 💎🏞️

☀️ Sky & Weather
- Sun, clouds, rain, or rainbow 🌞🌥️🌈
- Stars, moon, or night sky if your adventure is at night 🌙⭐

🎨 Extra Fun Ideas
- Magical bridges, floating islands, or secret doors 🌉🏝️🚪
- Colorful flowers, magical rocks, or sparkling water ✨🌸💧
- Anything else your imagination can dream up! 💭

🎉 JUNIOR EXPLORER CERTIFICATE

Congratulations, Junior Explorer! 🥇

You have completed your journey through mountains, rivers, lakes, and national parks. You have learned amazing facts, discovered wonders of the world, and explored the magic of nature and geography!
This certificate is awarded to:

FOR:
✅ Curiosity and love for learning
✅ Exploring the highest mountains, deepest lakes, longest rivers, and most beautiful parks
✅ Completing fun challenges and discoveries of our amazing planet 🌍

Awarded on: _____

Junior Explorer Badge: 🏔️🌊🌿

Keep exploring, drawing, coloring, and learning the world is full of adventures waiting for YOU! ✨

honeymoon